Once Upon A Dream

Geannie Alberti

Table of Contents

Acknowledgments 1

Chapter One: A Little Girl's Dream 3

Chapter Two: The Summit That Changed Everything 17

Chapter Three: Bridge Over Troubled Water 29

Chapter Four: The Work Begins 41

Chapter Five: Eyes Wide Open 49

Chapter Six: People Leave 57

Chapter Seven: Hope For You 65

Dedication

I dedicate this book to my Mom,

Elfriede, **Gertrud**, Elli Ziemski

Born: June 18, 1927 in Hamburg, Germany

Died: March 9, 1978 in Hamburg, Germany

She had one dream in her life:

To travel to Israel and see the promised land.

Despite everything that happened in her life, she was a woman of faith.

She wanted to walk where Jesus had walked the earth.

Her dream never came true for many reasons.

Thank you, Mom, for I am who I am because of you.

I love you always!

Acknowledgments

Kody Bateman, CEO and founder of Send Out Cards (SOC). Best-Selling Author of the book, *The Power of Human Connections.* Thank you for carrying the vision to make this world a better place by bringing mankind together. Because you followed your prompting, I finally found the place where I belong.

Jordan Adler, Eagle Affiliate with SOC. Best-Selling Author of the book, *Beach Money* and *Better than Beach Money.* Thank you for all the inspiration you bring into people's lives. Thank you for taking the cover photo right after you read the manuscript. I appreciate the gift of yours, being able to see through with your heart and create life changing moments! You are a true blessing to many!

My deepest gratitude goes to Kari Myroniuk, Executive Affiliate Partner with SOC, founder of Sassy Sisters Networking Organization. She reached out to me in kindness when I felt forgotten by everyone in this world. You lead me to SOC and I will be grateful for this for the rest of my life. Thank you, Kari.

Big thanks to my dear friend, Amy Kochek, ghostwriter and writing coach with Amy Kochek Kreative. You inspired me to write this book and guided me through the entire process.

Shana Rosenthal, Certified Consulting Hypnotist, Psychotherapist, Hypnotherapist, and NLP Practitioner.

Thank you for teaching me techniques and exercises that helped me through a very critical time. I am convinced that your help and support prepared me for making these important changes in my life.

CHAPTER ONE
A Little Girl's Dream

The sea was calm. The soft noise of the waves rolling on the shore was soothing. The air was filled with a strong, salty taste. The sun had just risen above the horizon and turned the ocean into a huge silver lake. I tried not to close my eyes while watching the sun rising because the scenery was so breathtakingly beautiful. With the windows wide open, I was sitting at a long breakfast table in an orphanage with another hundred kids my age. The building was right at the shore of an island called, "Wyk auf Föhr Germany."

This was not an ordinary orphanage. During the summer, they opened the facility to children of poor families from Germany's major cities for a summer camp. It was the first time in my life I saw the beach and the ocean, and I never forgot the picture I saw that morning. It was burned deep down in my heart for the rest of my life. I was 7 years old at the time, and my older brother and sister were there as well, but I was in the small kids' group. My siblings didn't want to hang out with their little sister. I felt lonely, confused and afraid of all the strange kids and leaders. We attended other poor family summer camps in different locations before. I used to hate them. This time, it was different.

The beach, the ocean, and the waves pulled me in like nothing else. Instead of playing with children, I preferred to be by myself, watching people or playing in the warm sand while I listened to the screaming of the seagulls flying overhead. I soaked in the salty air and collected seashells whenever I had a chance. I loved the feeling of the ocean water gliding over my feet. As young as I was, I knew that this was where I wanted to live when I grew up.

From that moment forward, the beach became the only place where I found rest and peace for my soul. And when I say the beach, I do not mean fancy hotels or watersports. I mean a place of safety, comfort, and acceptance. A place where I feel like I truly belong. The first time I saw the sun rising that day at the ocean, I felt like I became one with the water, the sun, the wind and the sand. At that very moment, a dream was born. A dream symbolically standing for a place of happiness and acceptance, a place of safety, a place to belong. A place where I would find love and people who would show me respect and kindness. A place where everything would be the exact opposite of what I knew. That day, I wished I could stay on the beach forever.

A dream was born in the heart of a 7 year old little girl, who had no clue what life would have in store for her and the journey it would take to see this dream come true.

On a warm, late spring day in Hamburg, Germany, where I grew up, my father took us children to an international garden show. Gardening was his hobby, and the show was free. We were so excited because it was a rare occasion for our family to visit places. My father was feeling generous that day and wanted to buy ice cream for us. I was so excited and joyfully shouted which flavor of ice cream I would like to have. I guess my father saw the prices, so he decided to get us the cheapest ice cream they had, which was Coca-Cola ice. I think I was 8 years old. I must have expressed my disappointment in a very emotional way, so my father slapped me hard on my face. My ice cream flew right across the sidewalk. My siblings were laughing, and my father yelled at me. He was very angry. I was shocked, hurt and confused. Years later, I still remember how I felt after this incident.

This became the story of my life. Every time I expressed what I wanted, it usually backfired on me. So, I learned early in life to stay put and stay quiet. At least, I used to try, but it did not work that well for me. It was just not in my nature. As you can imagine, I got clobbered quite often in life. Still, deep inside me, I was not willing to believe that this would be what life was all about. A driving force within told me, this is not everything. There must be more. Only, the "more" never showed up. Instead, at some point along the way, I began to notice that most people had a hard time when it came to dealing with emotions or emotional people. And I always was, and still am, very emotional.

My father grew up in an orphanage. When he reached his fourteenth birthday, he was forced to work on a farm. Then, World War II started, and he became a soldier to fight for his country. He couldn't have been any older than 20 years old, entering one of the most destructive wars the world has ever seen. After the war, he was a broken person, just like every other soldier who had survived. Being aware of his past made it easier for me to forgive him for the way he treated us, his family.

He was a controlling and abusive person. An environment of violence, immorality and alcohol encompassed my childhood. Sometimes he came home drunk. When we got lucky, he went straight into the basement to sleep off his intoxication. If not, he would become aggressive, beat up my brothers, throw the furniture around the house, or a list of other violent acts. I remember how we used to hide in the dark, hoping he would never come home.

My mother died when I was a young teenager from a brain tumor. She was the one who tried to keep the family together. As a young woman, my mom was diagnosed with Tuberculosis. At the time, this contagious disease was not easily cured. Catholic nuns hid her from the Nazis. Sick people with contagious diseases were considered unworthy, and they deported them to the concentration camps to be thrown into the gas chambers. My mother converted to the Catholic faith. After the war, she had surgery to remove the infected part of her lung. She was told not to become pregnant, or she would die during the pregnancy. Her Catholic faith did not allow birth control, and my mom ended up giving birth to 5 children. She had two miscarriages as well.

She was not a physically strong person. My father's lifestyle and her weak health condition left their marks. When I was 11 years old, I walked in on her while she was trying to hang herself. She broke down in my arms, bursting into tears and crying, "I cannot do it, I cannot do it!"

The day she was rushed to the hospital after breaking down on the street from the tumor perforation, was the last time I saw her alive. She went into a coma after the brain surgery. There was no sign of life in her anymore, and they decided to turn off the life support. I remember standing at her open grave at her funeral. I know I cried, but I do not remember how I felt.

With my mom's passing, I felt responsible for my father. I ran the household for him, took care of my younger siblings and tried to fill my mom's shoes. I was barely 16, and of course, I was overwhelmed. On one particularly difficult night, I was laying on my bed, crying my heart out because I realized this one fact, which followed me my entire life like a curse: There was nobody out there who really cared about me. I was alone on this planet. I decided that this was my reality, and I had to learn to live with it.

One night, my father came home drunk as usual. He was upset about something of little significance, and he threw me out of the house. There I was, standing on the streets of Hamburg, Germany, a minor, just 17 years old. Now what? Well, life left its mark.

As a young adult, I found myself in short-lived, abusive relationships. After being raped several times and consuming drugs to escape reality, I started to lose the part of my soul that was warm and friendly. I wrapped a shell around my heart and numbly walked through life.

It was the summer of 1980. I was about to go on my first vacation, since I started nursing school to become a nurse. My mom was a nurse as well as my older sister, so it was only natural for me to become one, too. Again, I had no clue that maybe there were other options. I did not know what I wanted. It just was not a part of my thinking. Ever since I can remember, I used to see peoples' needs or shortcomings and felt called to make a difference in their lives. This quickly became exhausting because people used to take advantage of it. But by the time I began to notice this, it was too late. As naïve as I was, I quickly believed what people told me. Actually, isn't this how it should be? But life did not work that way. Over and over again, I found myself in situations that were painful and sometimes even dangerous.

My vacation destination was Portugal in Southwest Europe. I traveled by hitch hiking together with my boyfriend. Of course, I was short on money. We both started nursing school the same year. The trip was amazing. We camped on the beach, had pineapple and garlic bread for breakfast and were dancing through life.

During this trip, we split up. We planned it this way from the beginning. He went to visit some relatives, and I continued hitchhiking. Very quickly, I found out that this was not what I thought it would be. The rest of my trip turned into a horrifying nightmare. On my own now, I was hitchhiking back home. I thought I could show the world that a young woman could do anything she wanted, but life proved me wrong. Being raped and robbed were some of the traumas I suffered on my way home.

There was one situation when I was not sure if I would make it out of a car alive. It came to the point where either he killed me, or I killed him. In the end, I managed to throw myself out of the moving car. I landed on the side of the road with no belongings, no money, and I still had more than 1000 miles to go to get home.

At that time of my life, everything I did seemed to end in chaos. My life was filled with so much drama all the time. It was exhausting. By the time I was 30, I felt older than I do now. When I jumped the 30 mark, something snapped. I started panicking about growing older. Because I never learned how to turn things around in my life, I made the same mistakes over and over again, wondering why I did not have any success at all.

In August of 1988, I married my first husband at a church we both attended in Germany. I was lonely and tired of all the toxic relationships I had been involved in. I thought I found a nice guy, and for the first time, I could make a relationship work. He turned out to be a homosexual and cheated on me with men during our 5 year marriage. This did not help my self-esteem, as you can easily imagine.

We got divorced, but we both stayed in the same church. Besides our counselors, nobody knew about the reason for the divorce. People judged me for it and felt sorry for him.

A Little Girl's Dream

During that time, divorce was not a common thing, especially when you were a member of a conservative church. It was never an option. I was considered a sinner and an outcast. People were talking about me behind my back all the time. Some were even rude and boldly yelled right in font my face what they were thinking of me.

I didn't have many friends in that church. Yet again, I thought I had to learn to live with it because I did not want to run away, not again. People expected this from me. "Look at Geannie. She is running away again, like always. She is a quitter. You can't rely on her." So, I wanted to prove them all wrong, only I did not do what would have been best for me, which was separating myself from people who did not have my best interests in mind.

Seven years later, I was still living in Germany and attending the same church. I married the pastor of this church after his first wife passed away two years earlier. All hell broke loose, and many people left the church because of our marriage. Actually, all churches in the city judged our marriage and spoke out against us publicly. This may be hard for Americans to understand, but in Europe, especially Germany, you can kill someone and be forgiven, but you cannot get divorced and remarry, especially if your spouse is a pastor. We were labeled as adulterers.

My second marriage already started on the wrong foot, and it was only the beginning. With my background and in my emotional condition, I submitted totally to my husband to limit the damage and the trouble. Again, I felt responsible for everything that went wrong. The church members, as well as the staff, had a hard time with someone like me becoming the leader of the church. From the moment I said, "I do," I knew this would be a rough road I was about to walk on. I just hoped that if we truly loved each other and stuck together, we would make it.

I did not see the warning signs. It took me 20 years to finally get the courage in my marriage to stand up and do what I thought was best for me. For twenty years, I tried to live somebody else's dream. I tried to make it my dream to gain approval and love. Deep down inside, I believed that if I succeeded, I would be able to fix my lost childhood. One thing I did not know back then was your lost childhood cannot be fixed. You can only change your future, not your past.

When I married my husband, I was convinced it was God guiding me. Today, I know I had a deep need for safety, and I believed this marriage would keep me safe. I was afraid of losing that safety if I left this man. Also, I was terrified by the feeling of guilt just thinking about breaking out and leaving this marriage. Fear is a tricky thing. The more it grows, the more real it becomes. My decisions were made from a wrong foundation, like getting married out of fear of not being able to be safe living by myself. Even though I did not dare walk away, deep in my heart I knew that the way this marriage turned out was never what I wanted in the first place. I put my needs last and tried to please everybody, until I found myself last in line almost all the time.

This marriage may have looked great on the outside, but on the inside it was destructive to my soul. I did not have the courage to walk away. The fact that I came from a broken background made it obvious to myself and others as well that the problems we faced were because I was not healed; I was too damaged; I had an anger problem; or maybe it was my jealous nature. For ten years, I tried to work on my issues, until I realized I will never be healed enough to make this work. Slowly, depression snuck up on me.

I found strength in the work of the ministry. This was my heart, my soul and my life, to serve people, reach out and change lives. I led the worship team and grew it to 50 members. In regards to ministry work, my husband and I were a great team. In ten years, we grew the church from 400 to almost 2000 members. We started a huge work to reach out to the homeless and drug addicted. We had several storefronts where they could get a meal, clothes, a bath and a haircut. I loved this kind of work. But, when things happened, and the ministry was taken from us, I fell into a deep crisis.

It was then that I realized we had no relationship outside of the church. My husband founded the church with his first wife. He was the head and leader of the church, and our marriage worked that way too. I had a strong desire to work on our marriage and to turn it into a partnership. This was not possible. We had two completely different personalities. The problem was not the strength and dominance of my husband but the lack of self-esteem and courage that I suffered from. I had no idea who I was and unaware of the strength that was inside me!

Meanwhile, we moved to Florida and took over a small church. The former pastor, a very good friend of my husband, passed away, and they asked us to lead the church. So we did. In addition to running the church, my husband found a new vision and work he pursued. I tried to be a part of it, but somehow there was no room for me. After a while, I saw that this was not what I wanted to do anyway. I became more and more depressed, wondering if this would be how the rest of my life would look.

It was almost 4 o'clock in the morning. I laid wide awake on my bed, staring at the old popcorn ceiling, thinking about how many times I wanted to paint that ceiling but never did. It was a clear and fresh typical Florida winter's night. I was watching the reflections of the full moon dancing on the pool through the mirror across the room. It was only two weeks until Christmas, but I had not started to put up decorations because nothing about today felt like Christmas. It was 2017, and we had been living in our ranch house in South Florida for 4 years. Every year, I put up nice Christmas decorations. It was a symbol of a whole and safe world to me. I loved the shiny lights and the beautiful ornaments. I had many angels in different sizes and colors that I set up. Always hoping, that maybe someday an angel would visit me and bring me some good news that would change my world.

This was supposed to be the most wonderful time of the year, but it was not to me. It made me so sad as I reminisced over a few memories that brought a little happiness into my life when I was a kid. My mom taught us how to sing classical Christmas carols in three-part harmony, and we sang a lot during the holidays. Singing was always a supernatural experience for me. When I sang, I felt like I escaped into another world of peace and complete freedom.

Just like every morning, I woke up with a severe migraine. My head was pounding. The pain was unbearable. The tension in my neck and shoulders were the worst during the morning hours. I tried to lie still, hoping the pain would stop; only it didn't. Like every morning, I debated with myself as to whether or not I should get up and face another day filled with loneliness and depression. I had to drag myself through most days, with the only hope of escaping my frustration being found in my bed for a few hours of sleep. The other option was to just stay in bed and feel sorry for myself. I used to drink wine at night, just enough to get sleepy, so I wouldn't think. Thinking meant realizing the truth about my life, and this pain was much more intense than the headaches in the morning.

CHAPTER TWO
The Summit That Changed Everything

About three years ago, I found out my dad had been diagnosed with cancer. The doctors gave him just a couple of months to live. The cancer was inoperable, especially at his age of 93 years old. I flew back to Germany to spend his last 3 months with him. I remember sitting on the plane, approaching the Frankfurt airport. I always felt like a stranger coming back to Germany. It was not my home anymore. There were two moments in my life that I remember well, when I felt so deeply in my soul that there was no place or person I belonged to. The first moment was the day my mom died. It was a terrifying and confusing day. With her passing, the need of belonging somewhere became overwhelming. It took more than 20 years for me to deal with this loss in my life. Second, was the moment my father threw me out. It became quite obvious that I no longer had a location I could call home anymore.

17

Still, my roots were in Germany. This was the place I was born. As I approached the airport, I became so sad that coming home would not be a joyful event, like it should be. The strange thing was, I never felt like an American either, even though I had been an official citizen for so many years. At the same time, I felt this fear of never, ever belonging anywhere. It was paralyzing. Sitting in the plane felt more comfortable to me than being on land, where I didn't belong anywhere. From my perspective, I was living in a nowhere land.

After my father passed, I came back to the states changed. When you witness someone leaving this earth, it completely shifts your perspective. The moment my father died, after a painful time of suffering, I experienced a deep respect for the gift of life. Something transformed inside of me. On one hand, I was mourning, but I was not really mourning the loss of my father. I was mourning the loss of the person I felt my father should have been to me. He should have made me feel safe. He should have been there for me. He should have been the one I belonged to when I was little. And I grieved this deep loss for quite some time.

On the other hand, I had this wonderful experience of closure. I chose to be with my father during his passing because I missed the chance when my mom died. I knew I had to do this. I did not do it to gain my father's love, which absolutely did not happen, even on his deathbed. But, I showed respect for him as a person based on my belief that no one should have to die alone. My prayer is that, on the day I am called home, I

The Summit That Changed Everything

will be surrounded by people who love me and will help me go on to the next journey.

Because my father was not there for me, I was searching and longing for this person who would make me feel safe and give me a sense of belonging. I thought, if I could find this hero, then I would be happy.

The lack of happiness that ran like a red line through my entire life led into deeper depression. I tried to find help and salvation in God, but through the years, the religious system created more fear and guilt in my life. When I first got saved, I was not even twenty years old. And no matter what church I turned to, I never really fit in. In general, the churches were structured and controlling back then. Today we would call it religious abuse. I think it was a tradition that would just not work anymore in the present time. Way later in life, I found love in God again, away from religious pressure and influence. But before I reached this freedom, I cannot count the number of times I asked myself the same question: Is this really all life has to offer?

I tried everything from meditation, prayer, inner healing through forgiveness, self support groups, counseling, yoga, hypnosis, healthy living, vitamins, fitness and countless hours spent reading every self-help book I could find. It all helped along the way, but none of it filled the deep inner emptiness and sadness I had been feeling for so many years.

At that time, my husband and I separated for different reasons. The religious organization I was a part of had become very destructive to me, so I walked away from it.

My husband was not in agreement with my decision, but he supported me financially. The so-called friends I knew for almost 20 years turned against me in a rude and mean way. I wondered how they could justify their behavior, when it was so starkly different from the teachings of their religion. I only had two options: staying and suffering while slowly dying on the inside or walking away from judgmental people. I deeply felt my responsibility before God to take care of myself, not just for my own happiness, but also for my physical health. Sadly, I realized nobody would stand with me. I knew deep inside that this was the right thing to do. I made my choice, and yet again, I was by myself.

At this point in my life, I was not only depressed, but I was also suffering physically. Around that time, I rescued three puppies. I thought this would help me emotionally to cope with my situation. But after several months, they started to fight each other until they drew blood. Instead of getting comfort from my dogs, they turned out to be aggressive. I started to be afraid of them. I didn't know what to do next. I educated myself and found out quickly, that the reason they became aggressive was because of my weak mental and physical condition. I did not provide strong pack leadership and that caused their aggressive behavior.

I had a decision to make. The dogs needed to go, or I had to change my life. The first choice was not an option, so I decided to get my life into balance. I sought counsel, started working out, and living healthy. After a couple of months, without any training whatsoever, my dogs behaved sweet and friendly again. I was so deeply impressed with this development. I then applied to the Animal Behavior College to become a dog trainer.

I started my dog training business after I studied for a year at the Animal Behavior College. It was an online study with 6 months hands on education with a local trainer, Wendy Kelly, an animal behaviorist and owner/founder of Pet Peeves dog training. She had 20 years experience, and I learned a lot from her. To me, she was the best teacher I could have.

A very long but lonely summer began. I had moved to Saint Petersburg, Florida, where I rode my motorcycle to my favorite place. All my equipment was on my back, and I was ready to spend the whole day studying in my classroom: the beach. After so many years of living other people's dreams, it felt great to do what I wanted to do.

Being a minister and wife for so long, I knew nothing about how to run a business successfully, but boy did I learn. I started networking with a group called Business Network International (BNI), the world largest networking organization.

BNI offered all kinds of training, which helped me learn and grow my business. I dreamed of building a dog-training ranch to rescue and train dogs that had no chance of adoption. I loved dog training, and I was good at it. Meanwhile, my husband purchased a 12 acre property. We reunited, and I was hoping that this could be a new beginning for us. With this piece of land, my dream to build a training ranch for dogs became more of a reality.

I quit BNI once I moved because of the long distance, and I focused on my business. It just did not work out. Falling back into old habits was slowly killing my dream, and the fire that was burning in my soul had no chance to shine. Life got in the way and things became worse than before. Now, I was really isolated, living in the country with no place to go or new friends to meet. The dogs saved me and kept me going. My dogs were the reason I got out of bed in the morning.

When I think back, I am quite sure that the work with the animals kept me from doing something drastic like suicide. I love to think that spelling DOG backwards is GOD, so God used the dogs I was working with to help me believe there was something worth living for.

When my husband and I reunited, I had my hopes set high to make our marriage work. It was the same year my father had passed, and I was still dealing with a lot of emotions. No matter how hard we tried to make things work, we just couldn't. To me, it felt like my marriage was finally broken, so I filed for divorce.

Shortly after this, my husband suffered a stroke, underwent open-heart surgery and experienced other complications along the way. The severity of his health caused me to reconsider, and I decided not to follow through with my plans. How could I? I

The Summit That Changed Everything

held on to the hope that the change in our situation could save our marriage, or so I thought. It was one of the first times in my life when I felt needed. Our financial situation was devastating, and looking back, I don't know how we made it through those years, but we did. Our marriage did not get any better. It existed only on paper. I really do not know if there was ever a time I felt more alone. My spirit was broken, my heart empty and my soul in deep depression. To get out of this isolation, I started networking for my dog training business again. It was terrifying to mingle, but I had no choice. I desperately needed to make money.

That's when I met Kari Myroniuk, Senior Manager of SendOutCards (SOC) and member of the women's networking group called SWAT: Successful Women Aligning Together. Dr. Robyn Spirtas founded this networking group and the main focus, besides growing your business within this organization, was creating a sisterhood that would help each other. I knew I had to break from the isolation I was in, and a women's group like that appeared to be a safe place for me. When I first joined, it was difficult for me to even talk to someone. I felt so rejected just by the way people were looking at me.

Kari approached me with gentle kindness, which I had not experienced in my life very often. She introduced me to SOC as a tool to grow my dog training business by sending my customers thank you cards, sometimes even attaching a gift, like brownies, to show appreciation. It only took a short time before I started seeing results from using this tool. My customers continued to do business with me after I intentionally connected with them through appreciation.

The great thing about this tool was I could order the cards from my phone or home computer, and the SOC company would print and send a real card to my customers' mailbox. I used to take pictures of the dogs I trained, put those pictures on the card, and the owner got a card with their own dog on the front of it. People loved them, and they spread the word. I also used SOC to stay in touch with my family overseas by sending holiday greetings or birthday cards. I fell in love with SOC the first time I heard Kari presenting at our networking group.

That day, I won the door prize of hers, and we got to talk after the meeting. I had such low self-esteem, but this woman was talking to me like I was her best friend. We bonded instantly. I thought this was because both of us came from Europe, but today I know it was the spirit of SOC, reaching out in kindness to people around you. And at that time, I needed someone reaching out to me, just the way she did. One week later, I got a cute card, saying, "You have been brownied!" And guess what came attached to the card? The SOC world famous brownies. I was blown away by the fact that somebody thought I would be worth it. The brownies were delicious. Believe it or not, I ate the entire thing instantly with tears in my eyes. It was a celebration for my soul. Shortly after that, we met, and I signed up as a customer. I used the SOC system for my dog-training business, and it grew twice its size in less than a year.

Kari and I became friends. She introduced me to her own networking group, Sassy Sisters, which was an informal group of sassy, savvy and successful women who are committed to building relationships, growing their businesses and helping others do the same.

After a short while, I became the hostess of one of the chapters. Being a hostess helped me overcome many of my fears. Kari continuously shared with me the value of becoming an affiliate with SOC. An affiliate is a distributor, who would share the SOC system with people who would like to become a customer or even a distributor as well. She was convinced that the residual and commission based income would help me financially, and in the long term, would create financial independence. I knew I desperately needed financial independence. The fear of getting overwhelmed appeared right in front of me like a huge mountain with no way around it, and I felt too weak to climb it. But more than that, I was afraid of being pulled into something I could not control.

After a little more than two years, I came to a point in my life where the financial and emotional pressure of my personal situation began to crush me. I knew something good needed to happen or I was going to break under the pressure. I shared my load with Kari, and yet again, she laid out in detail how becoming an affiliate with SOC could help solve my problems. Honestly, I had nothing to lose, and I could see in her life how SOC worked. I didn't know if I could be successful, but Kari helped me every step of the way.

Once Upon A Dream

The first step was to sign up, and I did. The second step was to meet Jules Price, a senior executive at SOC. I learned that in order to be successful, I would have to reach out to people and introduce them to SOC. And here is where the trouble began. I was so afraid of doing this. I just knew I could not talk to people about marketing. I was Geannie the dog trainer. The only thought dominating my brain was, "I will never be as professional as Jules or Kari."

After I signed up, I assumed that Kari would just leave me to go back to my life as normal. Wrong! Kari had just got started with me. She kept inviting me to an upcoming summit in Houston, Texas called Promptings Academy. I had never heard the word promptings before and didn't really think I would receive any value from attending. I had no money, no ambition and too many fears. The only thing was, through the years I had learned to be honest with myself, and I saw that I was trying to find excuses, which bothered me a lot. Each time we met, Kari brought up Houston: "Hi Geannie, how are you? The flights to Houston are cheap. The prices are ok for two nights at a hotel. You will love the people!" Kari did this because she knew me. She could see things I was not aware of, and I am glad she did. I was not convinced that I would love the people though. I was afraid of people. Still, I checked out the prices, and the flights were actually real cheap. I booked the trip, hoping I would not regret it.

Tom, Kari and I were on our flight to Houston. The plane started its descent, and I could see Houston from above.

26

Suddenly, all my excitement was gone, not just from the fear of flying, but by the view of a city that was marked by the last hurricane, which brought a catastrophic flood. The only thing I could think was: "What good could come out of this city?"

We arrived at the hotel where the summit would take place and where we booked our rooms as well. It was early in the afternoon, and Tom and Kari had a meeting to attend. My nerves and anxiety were out of control, as I observed people slowly filling the hotel lobby. The more people arrived, the more uncomfortable I became. I went to my room and waited for my friends to return. I must have fallen asleep when my phone rang. Kari and Tom were waiting for me in the lobby. We went out for dinner at a great Mexican restaurant and had a wonderful time.

We spent the rest of the night at the bar in our hotel. I was holding on to my glass of wine, hoping that nobody would talk to me. Kari and Tom were engaged in conversations and seemed to know all the people. I felt so vulnerable. If somebody would talk to me, I was afraid I might fall into tiny little pieces. Miraculously, people started talking to me, and I did not fall into pieces. Instead, I was overwhelmed by the friendliness I experienced. After a while, I really enjoyed the company while still holding on to my wine glass, just in case.

During the entire summit, I realized there were people walking this planet who are indeed interested in my success. Was this too good to be true? What I experienced here was something I had longed for and dreamed of my entire life. A place where I could feel safe and accepted. A place where I could feel that people really cared about me in this world. Could it be I was going to find this place in SOC? After 57 years of experiencing only judgment and rejection from people I was associated with, I had almost given up hope of finding real connections. It felt like magic to me. I was expecting at any time to wake up from a dream. Only, it was not a dream. It was real. I was about to enter a whole new world. It felt like I was walking barefoot on the beach, feeling the sand between my toes. It was the beach where I had seen the ocean for the first time in my life, and the sun was rising, pouring out her warmth and light all over me.

CHAPTER THREE
Bridge Over Troubled Water

The summit started on Saturday morning at 9 am in Houston, Texas. I was up very early, and I was not the only one. The hotel lobby filled up quickly with all summit attendees having their breakfast, walking around and talking to each other. A mixed smell of coffee, pancakes and bacon filled the room, and I could hear laughing coming from every corner. Some people dressed up, others liked to be more casual. Joy and expectation were hanging in the air. Everybody was ready to hear the latest from Kody Bateman, the CEO and founder of SOC.

I was about to hear a man who had the vision to make the world a better place by sending out heartfelt greeting cards, reaching out to people in kindness. To me, it sounded like a sales slogan. Honestly, when it came down to it, the main motivation was about making money, right? I had to admit to myself that this was one of the main reasons I was there. It felt awkward. I was doubtful and a bit critical, especially because Kari was praising him so highly. I quit lifting other people up a long time ago. It only led me to lower places, where it was very hard to get out of.

I was waiting and watching, ready to find something wrong, so I had a reason to leave. I recognized again this deep lack of trust in my heart. I asked myself, could it be true that there are people who wanted to do good without manipulating others? I deeply doubted this because my experience told me otherwise. Each time I dared to trust, I ended up getting hurt. I became a suspicious person, expecting only negative things coming from trusting people, especially men and people in authority. No matter how bad I got hurt in relationships with men when I was young, each time I started a new one, I trusted blindly. The end result was usually the same. They lied, cheated and broke promises.

I remember one of the first churches I belonged to. I think I was in my mid twenties, and I lived in Cologne, Germany. It was a Pentecostal church, and I sought counsel and shared my broken life's story. In order to be accepted, I needed to become a conservative and submissive church member. I tried so hard, but I was just not like that. I was wild, free and rebellious with a deep anger hidden inside. If you pushed the wrong button, I would explode. In the end, they threw me out of the church because I was involved in a relationship with a young man who was supposed to start a ministry career in that church.

Years later, I met the pastor of that church at a prayer meeting. He had walked away from his ministry. He recognized me and apologized for the way he treated me. I was deeply touched. Of course, I forgave him, but it did not undo the damage that it had caused. At every church I joined, I was unable to build real friendships or trust any advice that was given to me. Worshiping and singing kept my heart from getting bitter, even though I felt very isolated and lonely. I could tell many more stories like this.

I was sitting in the meeting room full of fear because I was not sure if I could survive another disappointment. It took all the strength I had left to come here. I trusted Kari when she said, "You will love the people." I was also full of expectation because I so badly wanted it to be true. I needed it to be true in order to hold on to my sanity. I don't think I could have handled another betrayal of my trust. I don't know what would have happened. Perhaps I would have fallen into a deep depression, started taking medications and checked myself out of life. There were two times in my life when I wanted to commit suicide. The first time was when I was 17, and the second time was when I was in my early 40's. Both times, I was too much of a coward to go through with it. And today, I am very happy that I decided not to do it.

Kody Bateman came on stage and to my surprise, he started teaching about "I am" statements. I expected him to teach on how to build and work the business to make more money. Instead, he was focusing on the mental health aspect of a person. He said, "The story of your mind becomes the story of your life." He got my attention. It all made sense. When I took a good look at myself, it was obvious. My old "I am" statement was, I am afraid. And the story of my life was, I am unhappy, lonely and unsuccessful. In the past, I heard and read a lot on positivity or proclaiming the good in faith. But the results did not show up. Today, it seemed to me as if I had heard this for the first time. It sank in.

The more I listened, the more I believed that everybody else is, but who and what was I? Kody had every one stand up and say the one thing that would hold them back from doing what they wanted to do. It was my turn, and all I could say was, "I am too German to succeed." Everybody was laughing. I felt so stupid. Quickly, I sat down trying to hide my face, while pretending to write something down. The next in line drew all the attention now, so I had time to breathe and sort out my feelings.

For the next exercise, we got some minutes to think about what action we could take that would change the first statement. I was thinking hard. Kody encouraged us to stand up and tell the audience our new "I am" statement. Without thinking, I raised my hand, stood up and shouted, "I am the path finder to happiness!" I could not believe I was doing this.

My heart was pounding, and I just stood there. Kody ran to my desk and looked into my face while pointing his finger at me. "You see? Germans can do it!" That moment hit me right in the middle of my heart. It felt like an electrical shock coarsed through me and a thick layer of ice on a frozen lake cracked in two.

Happiness floated all around my heart. Yes, that was me. I was the pathfinder to happiness. I reflected over my entire life in just seconds and realized that this was what I was always doing, or at least trying to do. I was always trying to find a way out of oppression into happiness. Could this be the turning point from running around and spinning my wheels to living the life of my dreams? What were my dreams anyway? I had no idea.

I welcomed the lunch break. I needed time to adjust to all these emotions. It was overwhelming and a bit exhausting for my taste. I thought, "OK, that's all I need. Let's go home now." I had no idea that this was just the beginning. If I would have known what was heading my way next, I would not have walked back into the room.

After the heart-changing experience, I felt more open toward what would come my way. They announced the next speaker, and Jordan Adler came on stage. Everybody seemed to like this guy a lot. He made some jokes, the atmosphere was light and I thought this could be fun. As Jordan started with his speech, Kari whispered into my ear, "He is an Eagle." Wow, whatever that meant. I had no clue. I thought it must have something to do with his last name. (Adler is the German word for eagle). Jordan shared stories of his childhood. Some of them were similar to mine. Especially the story about how Jordan and his best friend, Buddy, listened to all the Simon & Garfunkel songs.

They practiced the songs several times a week to perfect their skills. I did the same thing when I was a kid, only I had no best friend, Buddy. I played, learned and sang for and by myself. One more thing made our stories different: the outcome. Their story ended in the fulfillment of their dreams and mine did not. Jordan's friend dreamed of touring and playing music with Art Garfunkel. Many years later, this dream came true. I wanted to become a professional singer, and I wanted to learn to play the piano. I started writing songs and taught myself to play the guitar at a very young age. The first time I dared to sing one of my songs to my parents, they became so angry with me, and I was never allowed to get piano lessons. It killed my dream. I never stopped singing, but I stopped dreaming. The song I sang to my parents was about my longing for love. I guess they must have felt guilty and powerless to deal with my emotions. Everything life threw at me smashed one dream after another, until all my dreams were buried under sorrows, pain and fear.

As I listened to Jordan's teaching, suddenly all the happiness I experienced earlier disappeared. Instead, a dark melancholy covered my mind and heart. On the stage was a really cool and funny guy, telling his great stories, and I felt like I was stuck in the middle of this song:

Killing me softly with his song

He sang as if he knew me
In all my dark despair
And then he looked right through me
As if I wasn't there
I prayed that he would finish
But he just kept right on
Strumming my pain with his fingers
Singing my life with his words
Killing me softly with his song
Killing me softly with his song
Singing my whole life with his words
Killing me softly with his song*

As sad as I was, I felt anger rising in my heart. I was not far from running out of the room, when Jordan started to play a video clip with childhood pictures of him and his friend. The background music filled the room. Everyone was moved and listened. The song playing on the video was my song – "Bridge Over Troubled Water." I knew all the words forward and backward. I did not know how many millions of times I sang this song to myself when I was young while wishing, hoping and praying for this song to become a reality in my life. Thinking back, it was actually interesting that when I sang the song in the past, only the first and second verse left an emotional impact on me. Singing them helped me cope with the reality that I didn't have a friend to help me along the way.

---

* "Killing me Softly with His Song" lyrics by Norman Gimbel

Once Upon A Dream

Singing and delving into it helped me survive. I became the one who learned to comfort myself in those days with these lyrics.

When you're weary, feeling small (the way I felt on a daily basis)

When tears are in your eyes, I will dry them all (endless tears cried out in loneliness)

I'm on your side, oh when times get rough and friends just can't be found (times were rough all the time)

Like a bridge over troubled water, I will lay me down (dreaming of someone who would be there)

When your down and out, when you're on the street (17 years old, I was living on the streets)

When evenings fall so hard, I will comfort you (no comfort whatsoever)

I'll take your part, oh when darkness comes and pain is all around (endless pain with no one to help carry the load)

Like a bridge over troubled water, I will lay me down (dreaming of someone who would be there)

The third verse I sang of course, but I did not remember having emotions attached to this part until after this summit.

Sail on SilverGirl, sail on by

Your time has come to shine, all your dreams are on their way

See how they shine, oh and if you need a friend, I'm sailing right behind

Like a bridge over troubled water, I will ease your mind[*]

---

[*] "Bridge over Troubled Water" lyrics by Simon &Garfunkel

Bridge Over Troubled Water

I lived and survived many difficult situations, singing this song. It carried me through very tough times. The words were written in my heart. As long as I could think back, this was my deepest longing, to have a friend like that and belong somewhere. Tears started running down my face. I could not control it. I cried and cried. I was grieving the loss of a happy childhood that I never had, in a room full of people, and I totally did not care what anyone thought. The pain was deep and overwhelming, but it felt different this time. It felt like God used this entire presentation to heal my heart while ripping off the old bandage to clean the wound. I allowed the healing process deep inside. I wrapped myself into the music, and I felt safe.

Back on the plane, Kari, Tom and I were on our way home. This time, I did not sit with my friends. I got an upgrade given to me by the airline. Sitting in first class, I held my new, "Bridge Over Troubled Water" blanket tightly around me. It was a bumpy ride, but I could overcome the fear of flying easily this time. Something had changed, and I did not really know what it was. It did not matter.

Back at home, I sang this song every day. I sang it with or without a guitar. I sang along on YouTube and sang karaoke. I sang and sang. Two weeks later, I was singing my wonderful song, when something strange happened. While singing the third part of the song, I started to cry. Have you ever cried and tried to sing at the same time? Well, it did not work. I listened to the third part over and over as I went on crying.

Sail on Silver girl, sail on by

Your time has come to shine
All your dreams are on their way
See how they shine
And if you need a friend, I am sailing right behind
Like a bridge over troubled water I will ease your mind

And right there, it hit me like lightning. This was me! I am Silver Girl, and my dreams were on their way! What a moment! What a revelation! Waves of joy were running through me. I was doing the craziest happy dance in my living room. My dogs got so excited, they started dancing with me. You should have seen us, celebrating the new Silver Girl.

From that moment on, I had a new name. I called myself Silver Girl and told every body this story. I ordered a name tag so I could wear it proudly. I had a new "I am" statement, too:

"I am Silver Girl!"

Each time I said it, I felt my ability to dream come back to life, and I loved it. After a while, people started calling me Silver Girl. I loved saying it, and I loved hearing it. But most importantly, I started believing it. I dared to dream again, knowing they would come true. I wrote my dreams down from that day on. The pages got longer as I grew stronger. Now, when I was singing the song, the first two verses lost their painful impact. Finally, there was a road I could follow to get to the shining part of my life. Finally, the sun was shining on my life.

The April SOC convention in Salt Lake City was coming up, and there was no chance I could get the money together to attend. This time, the flight and hotel were not cheap. I was never really a go-getter, so my SOC business did not grow as fast as I wanted it to. But Silver Girl was awakened, and I started brainstorming ways I could get the money together. I decided to borrow the money, but who would have $1000 on the side to give to me? Kari did! I could not thank her enough. I booked my trip, and I was walking on clouds. Just like Kody said, "The convention begins the day you buy the ticket." I told everybody about my upcoming trip, whether they wanted to hear it or not.

The convention was beyond my expectations. It was a fest, a celebration of new things to come for me personally as well as for the company. A brand new SOC system was going to be launched on the first day. I was so excited. The energy through the entire event was at a very high level from the start to the end. So many speakers, success stories and testimonials left a deep impression on me. I learned so much. But most of all, I had gained a new self esteem, a new strength, and a brand new desire to follow my dreams. Here at this convention, I got all the motivation I needed to start building my SOC business to gain financial stability - something I thought would never be possible. To me, the leadership and the training of SOC have become this friend that would lay down for me like a bridge over troubled water. SOC became my family, where people were looking after me, celebrating my victories and comforting me in my defeats.

As we all know, the motivation that comes with conventions is not something you have every day. It was up to me to hold on to what I had experienced. Sending out the cards on a daily basis became my tool that kept me going. It was the tool that kept my heart involved, as I reached out to people every day in kindness. It was a constant reminder of why I was doing this. When people received my cards or gifts, they responded to me. They would share how deeply they were touched by it. In a way, it brought comfort to my soul. When I started SOC, you could say I lost my job of comforting myself and started comforting others. I was so glad I got fired from that job. My new job was my career with the SOC company, and the financial blessings would be the reward for following my dreams.

Finally, I learned what an SOC Eagle was. The Eagle rank was the highest rank you can achieve within the company. This year, there were several who had reached that level, and we celebrated their success during the SOC convention. On this day, I saw my leaders in a new light. With a deep respect and a heart full of love for them, I was so grateful to be a part of the SendOutCards family. When Kari said, "You will love the people," she was right. I changed my email-address to SilverGirlCards@gmail.com. Each time I write or receive an email, I'm reminded of who I am and why I am here.

CHAPTER FOUR
The Work Begins

The horizon in the east presented itself with its most beautiful colors. A deep purple slowly turned into a strong pink and orange and then became a wonderful blue sky that is common in Florida for that time of the year. The sun was about to rise, and it was already piercing its beams through the darkness. Another typical spring day was about to begin. I stepped out through the front door of my house and took a deep breath, inhaling the fresh, cool morning air. The wind was playing with my hair, softly touching my face as I overlooked the 12 acres of green pastures. The light breeze felt soothing on my skin.

My black feral cat named, Schwarzer Peter (black Peter), lied on top of my car, his favorite place. The soft fabric of the convertible top made a nice bed for him. He opened his eyes while tilting his head just enough to recognize me and went right back to sleep. I took another deep breath and started my usual one-hour power walk. Nobody was out at this time on a Sunday, and it felt like the world was all mine.

My thoughts went back to the convention in Salt Lake City. Almost a month had passed and everyday I realized the change that came with it was real, stable and lasting. A wave of happiness went through my body while walking my path. I barely noticed the 3 pound weights I was holding in each hand. I loved my morning walks. This time of the day belonged to me alone. From the distance, I could hear a rooster announcing the breaking of the dawn. I kept on walking while singing my favorite songs.

So many things had changed since I went to Houston. When I was a kid, everybody told me I was stupid, and I would never, ever achieve a thing. Unfortunately, I believed it. I allowed people to create a path for me, and I walked it. Through the years of my life, this habit became a fortress and kept me imprisoned for more than 50 years. Unbelievable, but it happens every day to so many people. I knew with everything I had been through and what I was learning right now, I could become a pathfinder to happiness for so many people. And I intended to do that. Until then, I kept practicing overcoming the rejection that came along with people's disagreements concerning the decisions I made or things I planned. I grew stronger with every day. It was not an easy task, but it was necessary in order to maintain my freedom and my happiness.

Another change I noticed was the way I felt around people. My self-esteem was stronger and I felt not only comfortable among people, but I could also relax and enjoy it. And this was new to me. It was easier going out and networking. I had goals that I now pursued, which gave me purpose and strength. The weekly training calls on Monday nights with Kody Bateman and Jordan Adler gave me guidelines and instructions. To the best of my ability, I tried to follow them and to my surprise, everything they taught me worked. The monthly gathering at Jules Prices' house and the meetings at the hotel that Jules arranged on a regular basis, offered great support and helped with my business challenges. And last but not least, the weekly team Zoom calls hosted by Kari brought assurance to my heart that my SOC business would be successful in every aspect - emotionally, spiritually and financially.

Every time I thought I learned my lesson, new difficulties appeared just around the corner that I didn't know I could handle. In the past, I would have backed down and quit. But with the team of trainers behind me and with the extra encouragement from Kari, I was able to get to the root of the problem so I could overcome, change and move forward.

I got better and better at sending out daily heartfelt cards, doing presentations, and having conversations. The shyness and fear slowly started to disappear. Sending cards to people I thought needed encouragement or just a friendly, "Hi! How are you," did something to me. When I felt the slightest approach of sadness, I looked through my contact list to send out a card. I found that when I reached out to help someone else, I received help for my own soul. In the past, I felt so lonely in this world. How many other people were out there feeling the same way? They just needed this one person to reach out and become the bridge over troubled water. By sending out the heartfelt cards, I could make this difference in people's lives. I could become that bridge saying, "You are not alone." A card could remind them they are not alone in this world. Someone is out there thinking of them, cheering them on. They are important to someone.

During the convention in Salt Lake City, Kody had special offers on campaign packages. As I mentioned earlier, I had to borrow the money to be able to attend the convention. There was no way I could afford these cards he was selling in the package. Again, I felt the frustration of not being free to do what I wanted, when I wanted because of the lack of finances. Oh, how I hated it.

Kody acted on a prompting and announced that if someone could not afford to purchase one of the packages, they should send him an email, and he would arrange something. Of course, I sent an email instantly that read something like this:

The Work Begins

Dear Kody,

I do not have the finances for purchasing the package you offered, but I sure do not want to leave the convention without it. I am on fire with SOC and the vision to make this world a better place by reaching out to people by sending heartfelt cards. I borrowed the money for the convention, and I canceled my summer vacation in order to be able to join BNI for a SOC seat.

Thank you,
Geannie Alberti
I am SilverGirl

After the lunch break, I headed to the reception. As soon as it was my turn, the friendly lady recognized me right away by my nametag. "Oh, you are Geannie Alberti! Come with me please." She led me to a special area where they had stored the packages. I was a little anxious. What was this all about? Right away, I felt this old distrust coming up. I felt guilty about sending the email. I felt insecure, and I expected to be corrected about whatever I might have done wrong. To my surprise, the lady said with a warm and friendly voice that Kody was moved by my email. I could tell she was touched by the whole scene. Kody decided to not only give me the entire package plus the card holder for free, but I could also pick ten more campaigns according to my goals and needs. I was overwhelmed by this kindness and tears filled my eyes. When I packed my suitcase, I was afraid it would be too heavy from all the goodies I got. There were indeed people walking this planet who wanted to do good. Motivated by gratitude, I sent Kody a thank you card.

This act of kindness was not an isolated event. It is something I have experienced over and over again ever since I started working with SOC. Over the years, I completely avoided taking risks because of fear that something bad would happen to me. Now I learned something brand new. It seemed like each time I took a risk, it was followed by a reward. It did not happen overnight, but each time I decided to do something that scared me, I was met with reassurance that I was going down the right path.

Of course, there were days when I thought, "I wish this would work like magic." Financial success did not happen over night. The day came when I got my first paycheck from the SOC company. To me, this was a milestone. From now on, it would only go forward, maybe slowly, but continuously forward.

When I came back from the convention in Salt Lake City, I dared to start looking at myself and my real condition, and I didn't like what I saw. I noticed that I compared myself to all the successful people I met at the convention and felt yet again, insecure. This old failure thing tried to hit me hard all over again. Will I ever be that successful? Those voices from my past that told me I was stupid tried to make a new entrance. But this time, I had leaders and friends, so I reached out. They were there for me, like a bridge over troubled water, to tell me I will be very successful, and I dared to dream again. I learned, through the training and the help of my friends, to go step by step. In the beginning, the steps were tiny, but they got bigger with time. I was going forward on my road to success in both my business and personal life.

Before I went to the convention, I purchased Jordan Adler's books *Beach Money* and *Better than Beach Money*. I took the books with me to the convention and asked Jordan to sign them. He wrote, "Dream big, Geannie!" And I read this every day. I could not yet write down things like space-traveler or having my own plane so I could fly places to rescue dogs. But I did have a vision of a dream that brought freedom to my soul and happiness to my heart while helping others to do the same. Nothing could stop me from going after it. Sure, I knew it was going to be a long journey. I was not in a hurry. I started with one step at a time. The joy that came along with this new life grew stronger by the day and empowered me.

CHAPTER FIVE
Eyes Wide Open

Somehow, deep inside, I never quit believing that somewhere there was a place where I could be safe to be just the way I am. I think that was the reason why, at this present time, I was ready to change my life from the inside out. It took 57 years to get to this point. I have come a long way.

Everything I learned since I started SOC helped me to stand up and proclaim who I am and what I want. For the first time in my life, I had the strength to step out of a role that I had lived my entire life. Growing up with a controlling father made me submissive to future partners. I had never learned to say "No" or set boundaries towards people in general without feeling guilty or beating myself up over it. I had never learned to choose for myself what I wanted or what was important to me. Instead, I tried so hard to please other people to gain their love and respect, which actually did not happen. It was a desperate state of mind that made me control and manipulate people to get what I thought I needed so badly. All that remained was emptiness.

When people control you, you will try to control other people. What I hated people doing to me, I did to others as well. People judged me, so I judged people the same way. This had become my automatic response. I was not even aware I was doing it. I only felt unhappiness and loneliness.

When I read Jordan Adler's book, Better than Beach Money, I realized that nothing would ever change unless I change it. The change that needed to take place was: "Geannie, cut the ropes that bind you to the ground and walk away. Be free!" I understood that I needed to recognize my ropes. Once I did that, it was easy to create a plan and follow through.

Still, it took a lot of courage. All those years, while trying to solve my problems, I was wondering why I was not able to change things in my life. I tried to fly while being tied up by my ropes. I could not see the many ropes that tied me to the ground. I was working on my flying skills so hard and got hurt again and again when I hit the ground.

Just recently, I listened to a training call about taking a leap of faith. I thought I took many leaps of faith in my life, but I knew that day, this would be the leap of faith that really mattered. It would break my habit of relying on other people for my wellbeing and happiness. After more than 20 years of relying on someone to take care of me, I knew it was time to take responsibility for my personal and financial situation. I did something I never thought I would have to do again in this life. I got a job, and I started working fulltime so I could support myself. The next step was to move into my own place and start a new life that would allow me to follow my dreams.

It was not as easy as it felt when I wrote it down. Considering that I had never in the past dared to stand up for myself, it took all my courage and strength from the moment I decided to walk out. It was an ongoing emotional process with lots of tears, doubts and fears. Remember, my deepest fear was that I would never belong to anyone or any place. Now, I was going back to renting a room and getting a paycheck every week. In that moment, everything felt like it was going backwards. Instead of being with somebody, I was all by myself. That was a scary thing.

Sometimes it is easier to endure and suffer instead of standing alone. The wonderful thing I discovered is, I was not lonely anymore. The friends that I gained through these last years were there for me. I had a vision and goals to go after. I had work to do. Besides my fulltime job, I was building my SOC business. I was busier than ever before. There was no time to feel sorry for myself.

Many times in the past I asked myself: "Is this all life has to offer?" The question I started asking now was more like this: "What do I want from this life?" I realized from that moment on that the possibilities are endless. It was all up to me. So, what exactly did I want out of life? It was easy to write about the past and everything that I did not want anymore. I realized that it was harder than I thought to figure out what I really wanted from life, now that I had all options ahead of me.

The most important thing for me was to gain financial independence. I knew I had to work on my job, until my SOC business could carry me. I arranged my work hours around my networking events so I could continue to get involved with many people. At this particular time, that was all I had to do, and I worked hard.

Through many conversations with my friends, I talked about the future. Where do I want to live? I realized, I could move anywhere I wanted to. This was an incredible feeling. When I listened to my inner voice, I heard: "Dream big, Silver Girl." I knew I wanted more than one place to live, just because of the fact that I love to travel. But the most important home I would call my own should be on the beach.

Presently, I'm working for a supermarket chain. But of course, this will only be temporary. What do I want to do? When I was in my early twenties, I started my education to become a nurse. First, it was because it ran in the family, but second, deep in my heart, I was a server. The deep feeling of sympathy could at some point really become overwhelming, if I would see people or animals suffer. I would call it my motivational gift from God. When I saw a need, I wanted to help. This was always a driving force within me. In the past, it was imbalanced because I never put myself ahead of others, especially when those people did not have the right intentions concerning my wellbeing. Being a minister for many years in Germany and in the U.S. was the perfect profession for my heart. I loved reaching out and helping people. At this point in my life, I know I will not go back to be a minister like I was before. I do not have to because I already am a minister with SendOutCards. The vision of Kody Bateman to make this world a better place by building relationships and sending out heartfelt cards everyday, to reach out to people and make a difference in their lives, will change the world. I have become a part of this ministry, and I am so proud of it.

The great thing about SOC is the fact that it actually is a ministry that financed itself. SOC is producing money. They do not need to collect money from the community in order to function. And in the long term, my SOC business will provide me with the finances for my ideas and projects I would love to bring into existence.

At my very first summit in Houston, Texas, I learned that I am a pathfinder to happiness. I found this path for myself, and I will make this my life's purpose to become this pathfinder to happiness for many other people, especially women who went through the same things I did. I am convinced that I going to write more books about this in the future.

There was still my passion for dogs. I will always be a dog trainer. What I learned through dog training and from the dogs I worked with was enormously valuable to me. I learned to live in the moment and not to worry about the future. I learned to break from my judgmental habit. Dogs do not judge. I learned to be more loving and kind. They love unconditionally and their loyalty towards their owner is beyond understanding. They are persistently pursuing their goal: the thing that is most rewarding to them, and they won't give up easily. Most dogs have more common sense than many people.

I had been in the dog training industry for almost 8 years, and my heart was always for the dogs that had no chance to get adopted because of bad circumstances. I would like to establish nationwide dog ranches on large properties, where I could rescue those kinds of dogs, give them proper care and training, and find them a home. Or, offer a humane place for them to finish their lives in peace and freedom. Through the work with dogs, I have learned to trust again. I would love to build a place where people with broken backgrounds could meet and work with dogs to learn how to trust again and receive love in return. I would like to get a pilot's license to fly small planes so I could bring the dogs to their new home.

Personally, these are some little dreams I would love to see come true:

I would love to meet Cesar Milan, the dog whisperer.

I would love to take piano and singing lessons.

I would love to learn some form of dancing. Flamenco would be nice. When I was a teenager, I was the dancing queen in the discos I went to.

I would love to have a pony.

I would love to travel the world and take many pictures.

Eyes Wide Open

I would love to go into space and take many pictures.

In order to see all of my dreams come true, I know I have to become a strong business builder and leader within the SOC family. This is the road ahead of me. This is the road I am going to follow. Everything else will just fall into place.

After everything I have learned, I know I will always reach out to people in kindness to offer help or comfort to people like me. This is who I am deep inside. This is who I am today, and this is who I will continue to be in the days to come. "I am kind!"

CHAPTER SIX
People Leave

When I was born, I was diagnosed with a certain blood disease, and I had to stay in the hospital for three more months. My mom had to leave to take care of the family. For the first three months of my life, I was alone in the hospital with no family attachment or care whatsoever.

I was told that I almost died in a fire that burned our house down when I was a baby. We were homeless and the three of us children lived in an orphanage for almost a year. There were two other accidents where I came close to death. Our family visited a place that was close to a railroad station, where older trains were stored. My siblings and I played among the trains, when suddenly one train started in motion, and I was standing right in its path. Seconds before it almost ran me over, my father rescued me. I certainly do not remember any of these incidents. The last one though, I remember. I was crawling under the couch to plug in a toy that needed power to operate and got hit by 220 volts of power coming from a damaged outlet. It was a miracle that I survived this accident.

All of the traumas above must have had an impact on a child's emotional condition. Realizing this, it makes absolute sense to me now that the anger and rebellion I expressed, even as a young child, were rooted in the fact that I did not feel safe and protected. Accidents happened. And when they did, it was a common reaction to find someone to blame for it. Subconsciously I must have done this, because I remember I always felt like I was being treated unfairly. I did not learn a social behavior that allowed me to make friends or build friendships that would remain. At an early age, people came and went. That was the way I experienced life.

Nevertheless, I had a hunger for life, and I remembered daydreaming about the day I could finally leave home and live the way I wanted to. I wanted to leave everything behind and search for my paradise. Well, we all know it did not work that way.

Somehow, the fact that my Mom had two miscarriages, one before I was born and the second after, made me feel special about my life and about myself. And I carried this feeling, no matter how bad it got. My father's drinking problem made our life very difficult. Many times, he drove drunk and lost his driver's license. We could not pay the fine, and he went to jail. Sometimes, he was gone for month.

People Leave

And then of course there was the big trauma that occurred when my mom died. The reason this trauma was extremely destructive was simple. The last time I saw my mom alive and healthy, she was visiting me while I was in boarding school. My siblings and I attended that school, which was 250 miles away from home. My mom was overwhelmed with us 5 children, and my father was just who he was. They both worked so they could pay for the school fee. I hated the school. It was led by Catholic nuns. The religious system was dominant and controlling. I remember waking up every morning in fear of what I might have done wrong the day before and how I would get punished. Many times, I cried on the phone with my parents, begging them to bring me back home. During one particular school year, there was a special event going on. I took a basic dance course, and all the parents were invited to come for the final ball celebration. I was so happy that my mom came. In the end though, there were the usual disagreements and moments of sadness, and we parted in anger. Shortly after this, she passed away. The guilt I felt symbolically buried me alive.

The same guilt followed me for the rest of my life. From that moment on, I felt guilty every time people left my life, regardless of the circumstances. I considered myself weak when I felt pain after losing a relationship. I also used to think people would do such things on purpose to hurt me. I learned later in life that most people are occupied with their own life and challenges. In general, many people would not take the time to think about how their actions would influence somebody else. That was not necessarily a bad thing. It was actually a big revelation for me because it brought circumstances into a new perspective and helped me sort my emotions towards other people's actions.

One thing that I learned as a young Christian was not to judge. Trust me, we judge more quickly than we think. Usually, it was an automatic reaction towards people or situations. During the years in the ministry, I worked very hard on my "not-to-judge" skills. But, it was during the years of training dogs, when I really learned how to avoid judgement. Dogs do not judge at all. Still, they are able to sense people's energy or intentions. I also learned that turning away from people who were destructive for me was not judging. It was pure self-respect. I learned to listen to my heart. If I could not let go of something people did to me, even though I walked away, there was a chance that I was holding on to judgment. Another thing I learned that became even more important to me was, not judging other people would not stop other people from judging me.

How can we protect ourselves from judgment of other people? The answer is simple: We cannot. The only way to gain freedom and peace in this area of life would be to reject and overcome the fear of getting hurt. The moment we realize that people judged us, we get hurt. Especially when those people play an important role in our lives. If you cannot let go of the fear of getting hurt, you will always remain a slave to other people's opinions and actions. I was the only person who could control whether I was a slave or a free person. This was very powerful! It would open the door to the path called happiness.

People Leave

And it did! I walked through that door, and guess what I found? Happiness! Have you ever noticed that judgmental people are usually very negative and unhappy? Just take a look and see for yourself.

The more I learned to set boundaries for people who used and hurt me in an on-going manner, the more room there was for me to just be myself. If you feel that you cannot be yourself in the presence of certain people, distance yourself from them. Cut them out of your life and move on. You sure can live without them. In fact, life will be more enjoyable without them.

There are two ways destructive people leave:

1. They come into your life. They consume what benefits their needs and leave as soon as they find something better.

2. They come into your life with the ambition to control you. Those people will not leave until you move on to a path they cannot follow. This path is called self-love and self-respect.

People who control you do not respect you. If you do not respect yourself and allow them to control you, you two have something in common, and it binds you together.

I had a feral cat living on my property. His name was Peter. I started feeding him, and he came back for more everyday. The moment I would stop offering food, he would simply go somewhere else. That was his nature. Controlling people are like my feral cat, Peter. Stop feeding them if you want to get rid of them!

In the past, I used to be afraid of letting people go. I would rather submit to suffering than take control of my own life and responsibility. The package of guilt became so heavy through the years, and it had a paralyzing side effect. I remember the first time I tried to break out of a destructive relationship with people who controlled me for many years. I had to move to a different city in order to stay strong and build my own life and business. Breaking free did not feel great in the beginning, because my brain, my heart and my soul needed some adjustment. Today, my feelings are in line with the person I have become. Now, it is not really hard to walk away from people that have a destructive influence on my life. Actually, I really do feel that I can be very proud of myself for coming this far.

Just let me make one thing perfectly clear. Not every person leaving your life is an abuser. People come, and people go. This is how life works. You meet people and sometimes you just go in different directions. If the friendship was healthy, there will always be beautiful memories and maybe even some contact later on down the road.

During my time in the ministry, I saw many people come and go. Still, every time a member left the church it hurt. Sometimes people left for personal reasons, but many times people left because of a disagreement according to changes made by the leadership. People did not like the changes. It made them feel uncomfortable, even unsafe. In order to operate a

People Leave

company or organization effectively, some changes are necessary and not always understood by everyone.

I joined SOC as an affiliate (distributor) at a time when the new system was launched. I already used SOC as a customer three years before that under the old system, which was quite confusing to me. I did not use it the way I use the new system today. Frankly, it made my life much easier. Other people experienced the system change differently and decided to leave SOC. This is absolutely OK.

It becomes complicated when people in leadership leave and try to take as many people with them as they possibly can. In my opinion, this would be wrong. Experience has taught me that there is no blessing in leaving in a way that brings damage or harm to the organization. I have seen this many times in my church. Sooner or later, we just reap what we have sown.

CHAPTER SEVEN
Hope For You

"The story of your mind becomes the story of your life." This is Kody Bateman's most famous saying. I experienced this truth in the past, but in a negative way. Feelings of fear, insecurity and guilt filled my mind, resulting in negative self-talk. This produced a lifestyle of emotional destruction, aborting any kind of success.

When I signed up as an affiliate with SendOutCards, I could feel deep inside that something new was about to come. The day I visited my first summit, everything changed. Why, after 57 years, did a change suddenly take place? It was not because of SendOutCards or people like Kody Bateman and Jordan Adler. They were like the kindling that lit the dying fire inside of me. Everything I needed to make this change was already inside of me. They just helped to reignite what was already there.

It was simply because I let go of the old and embraced the new, as I started thinking, speaking and believing differently than in the past. Yes, it was that powerful. It was a change I had been waiting for my whole life. A change I prayed for and had been waiting for someone to deliver to me. Then, I discovered this change was supposed to be made by me and me alone. The new experience was completely different. I started feeding my mind with self-confidence, hope and joy. The results were amazing. I started to enjoy life again. I was successful in almost everything I did.

I became a member of several different networking groups. In all the groups, I held a leadership position. It is now natural for me to interact with people. I work a full-time job while still building my SOC business. And, you are reading my first published book, which means I am an author now. And I have a dream, a plan and a strategy for my future. I have friends that love me and stand with me. And this is only the beginning.

SendOutCards delivered the tools, but it was up to me to use them in order to make this change happen. Still, everything I tried in the past did not get me these results. SendOutCards was so successful in delivering this message because the mission of the CEO and founder, Kody Bateman, was to bring mankind together by sending out kindness. This vision of being kind to others is my nature. SendOutCards just helped me to see that.

The most important lesson I have learned during this process is to love myself. The negative self-talk that used to automatically come out of my mouth, when I felt insecure or ashamed, got killed. Words like, "I am stupid" that I was told all the time when I was a kid, got killed. I killed them. Sometimes it still slips through my mouth, but then I just have to laugh about it. My life gave proof to my heart that the facts speak a completely different language. "I am smart. I am kind. I am successful." Those negative words had no power any longer over me. My entire life, I could not love myself. This was the greatest change of all. Now, when I look into the mirror, I see a kind, wonderful person ready to give her love to those in need of kindness by a word, an action, an email, a phone call, a text or maybe even a Facebook message. But most of all, I can share my love by sending a card with a kind and heartfelt message. And I made a promise to myself, now that I have learned to love myself. Instead of walking in anybody's shadow or settling for less, I will stand up and shine!

At this point, I would like to reach out to you, the one reading this book right now. Maybe you find yourself in a very similar situation. I would love to encourage you. It is never too late to change things in your life. I needed to go through every single situation in my life, and I do not regret one thing. Everything I have been through made me the person that I am today. I forgave people who did me wrong, and I asked for forgiveness for those I did wrong. At the time when I could not trust people, God sent me dogs to keep my heart soft. I always remember my mom's prayer for me, that God would protect my friendly heart.

Every pitfall and every time I failed, I learned a lesson and gained wisdom. Today, that helps me understand people and be patient with them. But one thing is for sure, if you are honest with yourself and seriously ready for a change, the right person will be there at the right time to reach out to you, to help and assist. Don't wait for people to do the change for you. I wasted too many years waiting, but nobody showed up saying: "Hey, girl. Here is the change you have been waiting for. Take it and be happy." Life does not work that way. The miracle is: You can do it and you are not alone.

If you have doubts, send me an email at silvergirlSOC@gmail.com, and I will respond. I was an impossible case, and I thought there was no hope and love for me. But there is hope out there. There is love out there, reaching out for you right now. Love is always there. It starts with you loving yourself. Others will love you because you know and feel that you are worth it. The people in my life I was relying on, like my parents or partners, were not able to show me their love in the way I needed it. So I figured I was not worth it. Now I know how wrong I was. I know and feel and breath being worthy of people loving me because I know who I am. I am kind. I am worthy. I am worthy to be loved! And you are too.

If you cannot see someone reaching out to you, start reaching out to someone who might need it. You could send this person a card with something uplifting written inside.

Hope For You

That's how it all started for me, sending out heartfelt cards to brighten someone's day.

Earlier this year, I met a woman at one of my networking groups. Her name was Anne-Marie Kelley. When we met, we connected instantly and became close friends. She told me her life story, and we had very similar backgrounds. I introduced her to my SOC friends, and I was hoping she would become part of this amazing family. Our friendship did not last long because she took her own life to end the heavy pain of depression. It deeply broke my heart that I was too late delivering the love to her that had changed my life. I cherished our friendship deeply, and it motivates me to reach out to people to make a difference. Loneliness is a huge challenge in our society. But there is hope. There are people walking this planet who want you to know you are not alone, and you are worthy of being loved.

Immortality

Written by: Larry Gibb

Performed by: Celine Dion

So this is who I am

And this is all I know

And I must choose to live

With all I can give

The spark that makes the power grow

And I will stand for my dream if I can

Symbol of my faith in who I am

But you are my only

I must follow down the road that lies ahead

I won't let my heart control my head

But you are my only

We don't say goodbye

We don't say goodbye

And I know what I got to be!

Immortality, I'll make my journey through eternity

I'll keep the memory of you and me inside

Fulfill your destiny, it's there within the child

My storms will never end, my fate is on the wind

The king of hearts, the joker's wild

We don't say goodbye

We don't say goodbye

I'll make them remember me

And I have found a dream that must come true

Every ounce of me will see it through

But you are my only

I'm sorry I don't have a roll for love to play

Hand over my heart I'll find my way

I will make them give to me

Immortality, **there is a vision and a fire in me**

I'll keep the memory of you and me inside

Manufactured by Amazon.ca
Bolton, ON